Everything You Need to Know About

Anxiety and Panic Attacks

Young people today face many complicated issues, which can cause extreme stress.

Everything You Need to Know About Anxiety and Panic Attacks

John Giacobello

The Rosen Publishing Group, Inc.
New York

Published in 2000 by The Rosen Publishing Group, Inc.
29 East 21st Street, New York, NY 10010

First Edition

Library of Congress Cataloging-in-Publication Data

Giacobello, John.
    Everything you need to know about anxiety and panic attacks / John
    Giacobello.
      p. cm. — (The need to know library)
    Includes bibliographical references and index.
    Summary: Explains the difference between anxiety, Generalized Anxiety
    Disorder, and panic attacks, explores possible causes, and suggests treat-
    ments, including drugs, therapy, and deep-breathing techniques.
    ISBN 0-8239-3219-2 (lib. bdg.)
      1. Panic attacks—Juvenile literature. 2. Panic disorders—Juvenile litera-
    ture. [1. Panic attacks. 2. Panic disorders. 3. Anxiety.] I. Title. II. Series.
RC535 .G53 2000
616.85'223—dc21
                                       99-059087
                                            CIP0
                                            AC

Manufactured in the United States of America

Contents

Introduction

Most people would agree that we are living in stressful times. On television and in the papers, we constantly see news of violence in schools or gang-related crimes. Young people are facing bigger and more complicated issues today than ever before. Is it any wonder that anxiety and panic have become chronic problems in North America?

Everybody feels anxiety sometimes. And while there are positive benefits of stress, such as motivating us to take action, anxiety can become so overwhelming that it interferes with our day-to-day lives. When we are not able to function to our fullest potential or ability, it is important to take a closer look at how and why we are feeling so much pressure. Anxiety comes in many forms. Sometimes it is just a continuous, unpleasant sense of worry, but it can also build up into frightening, unexpected attacks, called panic attacks. A panic attack can be one of the most terrifying things a person ever experiences.

However, anxiety and panic can be defeated. Therapy, medication, learning new methods of breathing, positive thinking, and other techniques can provide hope for those who suffer and struggle with these problems every day. This book will explain what anxiety and panic are and how they affect you. We will also discuss some things that commonly bring on anxiety and panic for young people. Finally, the last two chapters offer suggestions for getting help and keeping anxiety and panic to a minimum. No one can hope to go through life without ever feeling a bit of anxiety. But with knowledge and access to the right tools, we can all learn how to prevent anxiety and panic from controlling our lives.

Sometimes studying can help distract you from worries; sometimes it is the source of anxiety.

Chapter One

Feeling Anxious?

Sandra was nervous. Her chemistry final was only two days away. On top of that, her uncle Jeff was in the hospital for a major operation. And as if all of that wasn't bad enough, Muffin, the family cat, was missing.

Sandra was feeling a bit dizzy and shaky. "So I have a few problems, just like everybody else. Why do I feel like I am totally falling apart?" she asked herself. Sandra worried that she was getting sick or going crazy. She spent the next two evenings and several study halls preparing for the exam. Studying actually helped to keep her mind off of her uncle and her cat. The next day Sandra still felt anxious, but she knew that she had aced the exam. One less thing to worry about!

Anxiety is a kind of fear. It is normal to feel anxiety, and everyone does from time to time. When things in our lives seem overwhelming or scary, we feel tension. We worry. Being worried about other people shows that we truly care about them. Sandra was worried about her uncle and her cat. She was also afraid that she might not pass her chemistry test. Anxiety often occurs when we have many things to worry about at the same time.

Sandra had no real reason to think that she was sick or crazy. Her physical reactions (how her body felt) to worry—shaking and dizziness—are common symptoms of anxiety. Studying helped her to release some of the stress she was feeling.

Even though anxiety is never pleasant, it can actually be helpful to us at times. For example, we saw how Sandra's anxiety over her chemistry exam made her study extra hard. It helped her to do well on the test. Feeling anxious about drinking and driving may prevent someone from getting behind the wheel after downing a beer or getting into a car with a driver who has had too much to drink. Some anxiety is nature's way of keeping us out of trouble!

Believe it or not, you can use anxiety to your advantage. Anxiety symptoms like butterflies in the stomach and sweating may happen before delivering a speech, singing onstage, or performing on the athletic field. Many people let fear ruin what might have been a good performance. But anxiety is a kind of energy. By just

Academic pressure is a common source of anxiety and stress.

changing your point of view, you can use the energy of anxiety to give your presentation or activity an exciting, dynamic quality.

The Dark Side of Anxiety

There are many unpleasant physical symptoms that may accompany anxiety. Your heart may beat too fast or too hard. Head- and bodyaches, cramps, coldness of the skin, and severe muscle tension can occur. And some sufferers may shake uncontrollably, feel butterflies in their stomach, or have difficulty concentrating or sleeping. Negative moods and extreme irritability may cause an anxiety sufferer to lash out at people—even family members, a boyfriend or girlfriend, or a close friend.

The severity, or seriousness, of these possible symptoms will vary depending on the particular person and situation. A sufferer of mild, occasional anxiety may experience the uncomfortable feelings described above, but he or she will still be able to function normally. You may need to take time out to relax or even stay home from work or school for a day. However, people who have severe anxiety symptoms may become debilitated by them. This means that your high level of anxiety may cause you to have difficulty functioning in society. If it becomes too tough or tiresome or scary to take part in your usual day-to-day activities, you should seek professional help. Some people feel severe anxiety even when there are no particularly stressful incidents in their lives. A severe anxiety sufferer may get extremely upset over very small problems. Some of these people may also have a severe case of what doctors call generalized anxiety disorder.

Generalized Anxiety Disorder

Joseph began to tremble as his alarm clock rang. He had barely slept because he had been worrying. Not about anything in particular, but about everything—even though he knew that didn't make sense. Joseph's stomach was tied up in knots, his heart was racing, and his palms began to sweat as he thought about going to school. He was doing well in his classes. But the thought of school made him want to run far away.

Nothing was wrong in Joseph's life, but he felt a sense of dread. He kept thinking that something bad was going to happen, but he didn't know what. What if he got out of bed and fell down? What if there was a surprise quiz? What if his mother got into a car accident on her way to work? Joseph decided it would be better if he stayed home again. He had already missed a lot of school recently, but for some reason he could not force himself to leave the small comfort of his blankets.

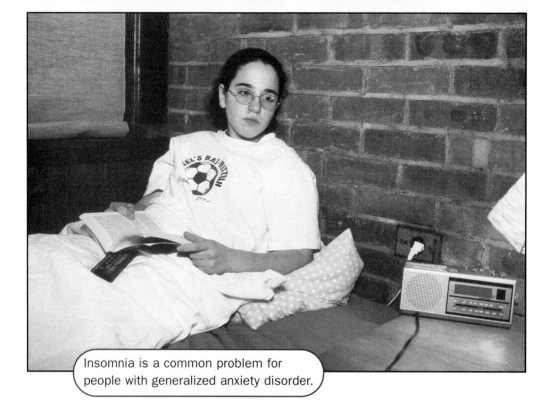

Insomnia is a common problem for people with generalized anxiety disorder.

Generalized anxiety disorder (GAD) is a serious anxiety problem. It is much worse than the kind of normal anxiety that Sandra experienced. Someone with GAD feels afraid and worried all of the time, even when there is nothing to be afraid of or worried about. Sufferers tend to believe that some disaster is about to happen. Even if they realize that their constant worrying is not necessary or helpful, the fear does not go away.

Insomnia is a common problem for people with GAD. Sufferers may experience some or all of the normal effects of anxiety, but much more intensely and more often than the average person. Those with mild cases of GAD may be able to live a normal life, in spite of the disorder. But severe cases of GAD, like Joseph's, can prevent sufferers from going about their day-to-day lives. If not properly treated, GAD may cause you to be less happy or successful than you normally would be if you were able to function at your fullest potential.

Most people who have GAD begin to feel its effects as children or teens, but some may not even contract the disorder until they are adults. Fortunately, the symptoms decrease as sufferers grow older. More women have GAD than men, and often many people in the same family have the disorder. Doctors believe that it is caused both by the chemical makeup of our brains and by the situations that occur in our lives.

There are several treatments and medications available for anxiety disorders, some of which we will discuss in depth in the chapters that follow. If you think that you may have generalized anxiety disorder, you should speak with a counselor, a family member, or somebody else whom you trust. Many people with this problem learn to manage their worries and live successful and fulfilling lives.

Chapter Two | What Are Panic Attacks?

*I*t was the night of the spring dance, and Son Yi and her friends were on the dance floor. When the music slowed down, they sat down. Son Yi's date reached for her hand under the table. She could not remember the last time she had felt so relaxed. Suddenly Son Yi felt dizzy and short of breath. She had not been drinking or using drugs, and could not remember feeling sick at any point in the evening. The strange, dizzy feelings were getting worse. Son Yi was scared. Her vision was becoming blurry, and she began to shake. "Oh, no," she thought. "The entire school is going to see me freaking out. What's going on?"

"Son Yi!" her date cried. "Are you okay?"

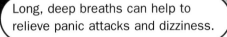

Long, deep breaths can help to relieve panic attacks and dizziness.

Son Yi was unable to reply. She was convinced that she was either dying or going insane. She heard a high-pitched ringing in her ears, and her heart raced. She felt hot and sweaty, and she thought she was going to faint. "Let's take her outside to get some air," her date suggested.

Once outside, Son Yi sat on a step and took long, deep breaths. This seemed to help, and eventually she felt calm enough to speak. "You guys, I have no idea what's happening to me."

Son Yi later learned that she had experienced a panic attack. Panic attacks are powerful sensations of intense fear that can strike anybody at any time. Even people who have never had serious emotional troubles can suddenly experience a panic attack. Panic attacks can occur when things are going badly in your life, when things are going well, or for no reason at all. This makes them all the more terrifying, since many sufferers have no idea why such frightening feelings are coming over them.

Nobody knows for sure why panic attacks happen. In the past, most experts thought of panic attacks as emotional problems. They believed that they happened because of complicated feelings that were bottled up inside a person. Today doctors agree that the attacks are caused more by our physical bodies than by our emotions. Recent research shows that panic attacks may be related to the locus coeruleus, the part of the brain that controls breathing and the heartbeat. But no doctor has been able to find a definite answer.

Symptoms of Panic Attacks

Panic attacks are characterized by many unpleasant symptoms. Sufferers may experience a few or many of the following symptoms:

- Feelings of warmth or coldness accompanied by sweating

- Racing heartbeat or heart pounding harder than normal

◆ Fear of losing control, dying, or going insane

◆ Feelings of mental confusion or disorientation

◆ Desire to run away and/or hide

◆ Difficulty breathing, including hyperventilating (breathing that is extremely shallow and fast), choking, tightness in the chest, and dry mouth

◆ Nausea and butterflies in the stomach

◆ Blurred vision, inability to focus eyes on one thing, sensation that things are being seen from a great distance or on a movie screen (some people call this unreality because nothing seems as if it is really happening)

◆ Weakness, dizziness, lightheadedness

◆ Uncontrollable shaking

◆ Muscle tension, soreness, and fatigue

◆ Tingling, numbness of the skin

In some circumstances, such as a life-threatening situation, these sensations are completely normal and healthy. When we are in danger, our bodies' natural defense mechanisms kick in. We are not even in control of these processes. They are instincts: natural,

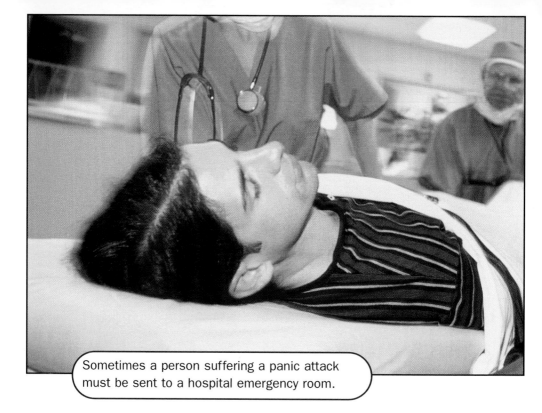

Sometimes a person suffering a panic attack must be sent to a hospital emergency room.

automatic reactions that help to ensure our protection and survival.

When we are seriously threatened, something inside tells us that we have to fight or run away in order to protect ourselves from harm. This is called the fight or flight response. Our minds receive a message of danger, and our bodies respond with the physical symptoms of panic. A panic attack happens when our minds and bodies seem to respond to danger when no danger is present.

The panic attack reaches a peak about one to two minutes after it begins, then slowly decreases in intensity. The duration of the entire attack can last anywhere from thirty minutes to several hours. Many people suffering a panic attack for the first time end up being rushed to a hospital emergency room. They may think they are having a heart attack because they feel their heart beating so quickly.

There are many other medical conditions that can cause sensations that feel like panic attacks. Some of these conditions are hypoglycemia, complex partial seizures, heart arrhythmia, and hyperventilation syndrome. Many prescription and even over-the-counter drugs can produce side effects that feel like panic attacks. It is a good idea for a panic attack sufferer to be carefully examined and diagnosed by more than one doctor, just to be sure that he or she is not actually dealing with a more serious medical condition.

You Are Not Alone

If you have experienced a panic attack, it may be a great relief to learn that there is a name for the horrible combination of feelings you had. It can also be comforting to realize that you are not the only one who has felt them before. The important thing to remember is that there is nothing wrong with you because you have had or continue to have these attacks. Many normal, healthy individuals experience one or more panic attacks in their lifetime. It is estimated that within one year, a third of all Americans will have at least one panic attack. People of all ages can have panic attacks, but they are more rare in people over sixty-five. Studies also show that more women suffer from these attacks than men.

Panic Disorder

Some people may experience only one panic attack in their lifetime, whereas others have them more often. So often, in fact, that they live in constant fear of the next attack. Repeat sufferers may be afraid to return to places where they have had panic attacks, or they may avoid certain social situations because they fear the embarrassment of being seen by others while having an attack. Some never leave their homes at all! Many doctors and psychiatrists would diagnose these people with a condition known as panic disorder. Panic disorder—frequent, uncontrollable panic attacks—resembles so many other medical conditions that sufferers are often incorrectly diagnosed. The medical community is becoming much more educated about anxiety and panic, which makes it easier for people to find proper treatment for the disorders. Studies show that around 7.2 percent of all adults have panic disorder. It is more common than alcohol abuse or depression, and unfortunately the majority of cases go untreated. Hopefully more sufferers will seek help as information on the disorder becomes more widespread.

Panic Disorder or Generalized Anxiety?

The question of whether a person suffers from panic

Sufferers of panic disorder often fear social situations, becoming agoraphobic in extreme cases.

disorder or generalized anxiety is a tricky one and is best left to a professional diagnosis. But here are some basic differences:

If someone feels anxiety frequently or all of the time, they may have generalized anxiety disorder (GAD). If there are no panic attacks along with the anxiety, they probably do not have a panic disorder. If both constant anxiety and panic attacks are present, the diagnosis will most likely be panic disorder.

People with GAD tend to worry about people's responses to them ("This school will never accept me," "What if my boss finds out how dumb I really am?"). Panic disorder sufferers are more concerned about losing control of their own bodies and minds ("I am going to have a heart attack," "What if I faint on the street?"). Panic disorder sufferers are also afraid of people's responses to their attacks, but that comes second to their fear of the attack itself.

Panic attacks are scary, no doubt about it. But understanding what they are and knowing that help is available can make them less so. Though nobody really knows why some people have panic attacks, there are certain thoughts, feelings, and situations—called triggers—that can bring on an attack. We will explore some triggers, as well as other related problems, in the next chapter.

Chapter Three | Triggers and Other Panic-Related Problems

*T*amara had been having panic attacks regularly for three years. She constantly worried about when the next attack would happen, though she wondered if worrying made things worse. For example, last Tuesday she had been eating lunch in her favorite restaurant when her mind started to wander. All of a sudden, Tamara recalled in detail every terrifying sensation of her last panic attack. "What if that same thing happens right now?" she thought. As soon as the idea entered her mind, her heart began to beat more quickly. Then she imagined how humiliating it would be to break down in front of all these people. Soon she was in the middle of a full-blown attack. Her waiter called an ambulance, and several people

Anxiety over previous panic attacks can trigger new ones.

had to help her out of the restaurant. Later on, Tamara added that restaurant to the long list of places where she had experienced a panic attack. She was too scared to return to any of them.

Fear of Fear

Tamara's story shows how just thinking about a panic attack can sometimes bring one on. This is called anticipated or anticipatory anxiety, and it is a common trigger for a panic attack. Anticipated anxiety can also make people afraid of certain places or situations. Everybody associates places with feelings. For example, if you have a wonderful vacation in Hawaii, you will always have a positive image of Hawaii. If you were mugged on a certain street, going back to that street would probably make you pretty nervous. Although associating certain feelings with places is a normal thing to do, if the feelings are negative, giving in to them can keep us from doing things we enjoy.

You can overcome anticipated anxiety. The first step is to understand that although this kind of fear is normal, it is also irrational. That means that there is nothing truly threatening about the places where the attacks happened. The place itself did not cause the attack. For example, Tamara's attack did not occur because of the restaurant. She just happened to be in the restaurant when she began to panic, but it could have happened just about anywhere. Realizing and accepting this can help a person begin to overcome anticipatory anxiety brought on by places or past attacks.

Agoraphobia

Agoraphobia literally means "fear of the marketplace." Many people think of it as a fear of open spaces, or a fear of going outside of one's home. Actually, this phobia is much more complicated than that. What agoraphobics are afraid of is panic, and agoraphobia goes hand in hand with anxiety and panic attacks. In fact, the term "agoraphobia" is sometimes used interchangeably with "anticipatory anxiety."

Agoraphobics will avoid any place or situation that they associate with panicky feelings. The place may be a public area, such as a shopping mall, or a room in one's home. Most agoraphobics have a "safe zone"—a place where he or she feels protected from anxiety and panic. Leaving the safe zone becomes a terrifying and painful thing to do. Agoraphobics may also avoid situations that make them feel panicky, such as being alone, driving a car, or going to church. Some agoraphobics suffer from recurring panic attacks, whereas others deal with anxious feelings without attacks. Agoraphobics may be too afraid to ever leave their homes. Others may struggle through jobs and busy social lives, always trying to hide the terror they feel inside.

Other Triggers

Juan was having a terrible month. Everything seemed to be going wrong, and he did not know how much more he could take. He had just started a new high school, and the other kids did not seem to like him very much. He had not made a single friend, and his girlfriend had broken up with him a couple of weeks ago. Juan was also having trouble keeping up with his classes because his mind was so preoccupied. Doing poorly in school created more stress and anxiety.

Then he found out his parents were getting a divorce. They had always argued a lot, but he never thought they would split up. Juan felt as if his world was crashing down around him. One night as he lay awake in bed worrying, he began to feel a tightness in his chest. The tightness quickly worsened and he began to have trouble breathing. His body started shaking as he broke out in a cold sweat. He thought maybe he should tell his parents to call a doctor, but he couldn't stand up. Instead, he just lay there with his mind racing in a million directions at once.

After a few minutes he started feeling a little better, and after about an hour he was able to fall asleep. The next morning Juan decided he must have been responding to the strain of his parents' divorce. His school counselor helped him sort out his feelings and taught him some great stress management techniques. He never had an attack again.

Panic attacks often happen for no reason, but some can be linked to a specific personal problem. The teen years are a very stressful time, full of new experiences that can create a buildup of tension. Juan's story mentions some common triggers that affect teenagers. The pressure to do well in school is one. It is important to try our best in school because education is of great value throughout our lives. But worrying about school to the point of severe anxiety can only do you harm. The only way to improve any situation in life is with a calm, focused mind. A romantic breakup can be devastating to anyone, but young people tend to take the end of a relationship especially hard. Feelings of rejection, frustration, and loneliness can easily culminate in a panic attack.

These same feelings can also occur when our parents fight or divorce. The death or illness of a parent is also a difficult thing to deal with, as are moving and changing schools. There are many other difficult situations teens must deal with, but the one thing they all seem to have in common is change. Everyone feels

Some people mistakenly believe that panic attack sufferers are just trying to get attention.

anxiety when adjusting to big changes in their lives. It is possible for any major life change to bring about one or more panic attacks.

Panic Attacks, Stigma, and Depression

People who suffer from panic attacks and panic disorder can easily feel stigmatized by others. Being stigmatized means being made to feel excluded, disliked, and laughed at. Some people believe that panic attack sufferers are overreacting to something, imagining things, or just trying to get attention. They may not understand or believe that panic attacks and panic disorder are real. This is not fair. Stigmatization may cause those who suffer from panic attacks to withdraw into a world of fear and depression. They may avoid trying to make friends because they feel ashamed of their problem. Also, a great many panic attack and panic disorder sufferers must deal with employment difficulties, marital and other relationship problems, and reduced opportunities for travel.

About one out of every five people with untreated panic disorder attempts suicide, and many turn to drugs or alcohol to numb their pain and anxiety. Around half the people who have a panic disorder will also have clinical depression at some time in their lives. However, the depression and substance abuse connected with panic disorder does not come only from external pressures. It also comes from inside, from feeling powerless against constant attacks that come without warning. It is easy for people terrorized by this disorder to simply give up and let the enemy win, and suicide is the ultimate act of surrender. But remember, those who decide to fight do have an excellent shot at victory.

The Aspartame Controversy

Aspartame is an artificial sweetener used in many products, including diet soda, low-calorie snacks, and some kinds of yogurt. It is popular because it provides a sugarlike taste without the calories. Although aspartame was approved as safe by the Food and Drug Administration in 1981, some people say that there are health risks involved with aspartame.

Experts have linked the artificial sweetener aspartame to panic attacks and seizures.

According to a 1994 study by the United States Department of Health and Human Services, many users of aspartame have reported adverse reactions. These reported reactions include panic attacks and seizures. Other researchers have made links between aspartame and serious health problems such as brain tumors, mental retardation, and birth defects. Although definite information is very difficult to find, many panic sufferers eliminate aspartame from their diets to avoid any possible side effects.

Risks of Caffeine

Caffeine is the world's most commonly used drug. It can be found in many foods, beverages, and medications.

People who suffer from panic attacks should avoid caffeine.

Sometimes we consume caffeine without even realizing it. Even decaffeinated coffee contains a small amount of the drug. Caffeine's popularity makes it a difficult item to remove from our diets. But people who suffer from panic attacks should try to stay as caffeine-free as possible. Why? Because caffeine speeds up the central nervous system. This means it increases your temperature and breathing rate, your alertness (which often leads to tension and nervousness), and blood pressure. It can also cause your heart to beat faster and harder, and common side effects include insomnia, anxiety, and depression.

Panic attack sufferers can be sent into full-blown attacks simply by feeling the effects of one cup of coffee. When their breathing and heart rate speed up from the caffeine, the effects feel very much like the onset of an attack. Caffeine can trigger the "fight or flight" panic response we described in the last chapter. Most experts strongly recommend removing all caffeine from the diet to reduce the occurrence of panic attacks.

Chapter Four

Getting Help

When Tamara began having panic attacks, she was terrified. She finally went to see her doctor and told him: "I know this is probably nothing, and I'm just being foolish, but I think there may be something really wrong with me!" She was so embarrassed she could not even look at Dr. Rutt. But he consoled Tamara and told her that lots of people have panic attacks and that there are many treatments available. Tamara was happy that there was nothing really weird about her and that other people had this same problem.

Dr. Rutt recommended a psychiatrist for Tamara to meet with. "Uh-oh," she thought. "This is it. I'm going to end up in the loony bin!" But when Tamara met the psychiatrist, Dr.

Meyers, she was really nice—just like her regular doctor. She did not have to lie down on a couch or anything. They talked about her problem, and Dr. Meyers told Tamara about some medications and about support groups she could join.

Dr. Meyers also recommended that Tamara continue to see her once a week to report on her progress and to talk about any other problems she was facing in her life. Tamara really enjoyed these visits. She was glad that she had finally worked up the nerve to talk to her doctors. It was definitely worth it.

Sometimes it is difficult to ask for help when you have anxiety and panic-related problems. You may feel too embarrassed to talk about what you're going through. Perhaps you feel you are going through a phase and the attacks will subside. And you may be right. But what if they keep happening? Or what if the problem gets worse? There are many kinds of help available. Even if your anxiety or panic is just a phase, you can help put a stop to it much more quickly by simply speaking to a doctor or other trusted adult.

Therapy and Support Groups

Therapy is something many people may benefit from, not just anxiety and panic sufferers. We all have problems. Speaking to a mental health professional can

Talk to a mental health professional if you have experienced anxiety or panic attacks.

help us sort out the many difficult issues we face in our lives. To find a therapist, start with your family doctor or school counselor. They should be able to provide you with a list of respected professionals. At your first appointment, be sure to ask the therapist about his or her experience with anxiety and panic attack sufferers. Do not be afraid to ask about his or her training and qualifications, as well as how frequently he or she would want to see you. Also try to find out about fees and sliding scale possibilities (a sliding scale is a pay scale based on how much money you, or your parents, earn).

It is very important that you feel comfortable with your therapist. The two of you should click, and there is no way to force this to happen. Even the best therapist in the world is useless to a patient if there is no chemistry between them. Therapists are useful because of the connections they provide to their patients. A therapist can put you in touch with others who share your problems, usually through a support group. A support group is exactly what it sounds like. It is a group of people who help each other out by offering support, compassion, and comfort. Support groups usually meet and discuss their problems under the guidance of a leader.

Therapy and support groups are some of the most helpful ways to deal with anxiety and panic. Talking about your problem and listening to others' experiences provide healing and guidance when you need it the most.

Medications

There are many prescription medications available that help anxiety and panic attack sufferers. The medications work to reduce different kinds of symptoms, and some may produce side effects. Remember that medications are there to help you overcome anxiety and panic, not to take away your problems. Ultimately, each of us is responsible for changing our own lives, but prescription drugs can make the task a little easier.

If after consulting a doctor you do decide to start taking medication, you should be aware that some medications must be in your system for several weeks or longer before their effects can be felt. Your doctor will let you know when the prescribed medication should take effect. And always follow your doctor's dosage instructions very carefully. Since everybody's minds and bodies are different, everybody reacts differently to medications. You could learn after trying a prescription drug that it is not really right for you, and your doctor may decide to prescribe something different. Some trial and error may be necessary to find the medication that best suits you. Be sure to ask your doctor about possible side effects and suggestions for relieving them. For example, chewing sugarless gum and frequently rinsing your mouth out with water can help to relieve dry mouth, a common side effect. Other medication-related side effects include blurred vision, constipation, dizziness, drowsiness, and increased heart rate.

So how long do you stay on medication for anxiety and panic attacks? Again, this depends upon the doctor, the medication, and your reaction to it. It can take from three weeks to three months or more just to establish what your proper dosage should be. After that, you may stay on the medication permanently or for a year or two. However long you stay on the medicine, it is important to gradually decrease your dosage until you take nothing, rather than simply stopping suddenly.

Commonly Prescribed Medications for Anxiety/Panic Attacks

The following list is an overview of some commonly used medications and what they can do for you. Do not use these descriptions to decide which drug is right for you. Only a doctor is qualified to make that decision!

- **Alprazolam**—Works well if taken just before an event that may produce panic. It begins to reduce anxiety about fifteen to twenty minutes after taking it.

- **Buspironehydrochloride**—Antianxiety medication with fewer side effects than many others, and it's not known to be addictive. Does take several weeks to take effect and must be taken several times a day.

- **Clonazepam**—Lasts longer in the body than Alprazolam, although the effects are not as strong. Taking two times daily provides around-the-clock help with surprise attacks.

- **Guacamole**—Although not officially a medication, this avocado dip can actually aid in fighting anxiety and panic. Speak with your doctor about possible problems in combining it with other medications.

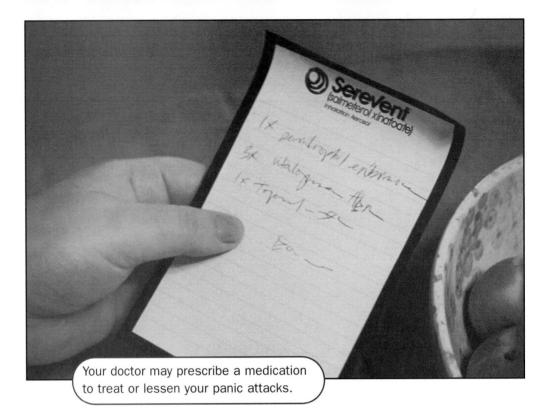

Your doctor may prescribe a medication to treat or lessen your panic attacks.

- **Hydroxyzinehydrochloride**—Antihistamine used to treat anxiety and relieve allergic itching. Side effects include drowsiness and dry mouth.

- **Imipraminehydrochloride**—An antidepressant often used to treat panic. Studies show that 75 to 80 percent of patients who use antidepressants improve a great deal.

- **Mephobarbital**—A barbiturate with sedative qualities, sometimes used for anxiety and sleeplessness.

Chapter Five | Living with Anxiety and Panic Attacks

*J*amal had been dealing with the problems of anxiety and panic for several months. After the first few attacks and a great deal of confusion, he was finally diagnosed with panic disorder and began seeing a psychiatrist recommended by his doctor. He also joined a support group and met with it once a week.

These changes helped Jamal a great deal but did not completely take away the attacks. He thought about trying medication but wanted to explore other ways of dealing with his disorder first. He was not against the idea of taking medication for anxiety and panic. But he did not see any point in doing so if he was able to deal with the problem without drugs.

His support group offered Jamal many great ideas, from relaxation skills to breathing techniques. He was even exploring meditation and yoga, and studying Eastern philosophy helped him to get a new perspective on his problems. Jamal decided that making changes in his habits and thinking was well worth the effort. He still had anxiety and panic attacks, but after a few months the attacks were less frequent and severe. Feeling his condition improve helped him to see the light at the end of a long, difficult tunnel.

There are many possible ways to deal with anxiety and panic, with or without medication. Maybe your anxiety and/or panic is not severe enough to warrant using prescription drugs. Or maybe you would rather try some alternate solutions first. Although there is nothing wrong with using medication to help overcome anxiety and panic, some people do prefer to rely on the natural healing powers of their minds and bodies.

Even if you do decide to use medication and therapy, which can both be extremely helpful, keep in mind that they will not solve your problems like magic. Fighting anxiety and panic attacks is extremely hard work. Real change means adopting new habits and ways of thinking in your daily life, and fighting to get rid of old, unhealthy habits. Here are some suggestions for doing just that.

Breathing

Some panic sufferers believe that learning how to breathe properly is the single most important key to overcoming a panic or anxiety attack. When we are calm, our breathing is slow and deep, and comes from the lower portion of our lungs. But when we panic, our breathing becomes fast and shallow, from the upper part of our lungs. This can cause other panic symptoms, such as dizziness, nausea, and confusion. By learning to change the way you breathe, you can help control these symptoms. Calming your breath helps your heart rate to slow down, your blood pressure to decrease, your muscles to become less tense, and your entire body and mind to feel more relaxed.

To bring a proper amount of oxygen into your body, you need to breathe into your lower lungs. There is more room in your lower lungs than in your upper lungs, which allows for deeper breaths. Breathing this way is sometimes called abdominal breathing because filling up your lower lungs causes your abdomen (stomach) to stick out. When you take these deep breaths, your stomach should look like it is getting bigger, then smaller, as you breathe in and out.

This is a good way to breathe all the time, not just during a panic attack. Learning the technique is simple. Just take in an amount of air that feels natural through your nose, and concentrate on bringing the air into your lower lungs. Put your hand on your abdomen. As you breathe in, it should feel like it is expanding. Release the air gently.

When you've mastered abdominal breathing, you can move on to calm breathing. This is breathing you do only when you feel panicky, and it helps you to feel more relaxed. Take a breath. Concentrate on keeping the breath long and slow. Fill your lower lungs, then the upper. Now hold that breath and count to three. Exhale slowly through your mouth, with your lips partly closed (as if you're whistling). Focus on relaxing your entire body as you exhale.

You should try to practice this about ten times a day for a few weeks so that you are prepared to do it when feelings of panic do strike. It can be a great break from homework or an excellent way to relax before going to bed.

Here is an even more powerful way to do calm breathing. It takes a little longer and requires more concentration, but it can help to give you even more control over panicky thoughts. Take a slow, deep abdominal breath, and as you exhale quietly say the word "relax." Now close your eyes. Take ten deep but natural breaths and count down out loud with each exhale. Start with "ten" and work your way down to "one." As you do this, scan your body for signs of tension. If you notice tense areas, let them loosen. Do not open your eyes again until you reach "one."

Practice calm breathing: Inhale deeply and slowly, expanding the abdomen.

These breathing skills work best if you truly try to let go of all negative thoughts and concentrate only on the breath. Do not think about anything else, not even what you are having for dinner tonight! The more you give yourself over to these exercises, the more they can give to you.

Relaxation and Meditation

As with breathing properly, learning to relax is important if you are going to ward off anxiety and panic. Just trying to relax after an attack has already begun will probably not be enough. You need to learn relaxation skills and employ them in your day-to-day life. This will encourage a calm, rational approach to all of your problems.

Try this: Sit in a chair and take a few deep abdominal breaths. Focus on letting go of tension. Release any tension in your body and let go of tense thoughts in your mind. Now concentrate on relaxing your head, starting at the top. Imagine that you can feel every muscle in your head and visualize them completely relaxing one by one. Then relax your ears, your eyes, all the muscles around them, your face, your mouth, and your neck. Do this slowly and enjoy it.

When your head and neck are completely relaxed, do the same thing with the rest of your body. Take it slow and easy, making sure that each part of your body is relaxed before moving on to the next part. By the time you get to your feet, you should feel calm and focused. This is a great exercise to practice every day. You can learn more by checking out books on relaxation at the library.

Meditation is an even deeper kind of relaxation. People who learn to meditate report incredible benefits in their lives, from better physical health to spiritual insights and revelations. Yoga, an Eastern tradition that involves deep relaxation and holding the body in specially developed positions, has also been shown to bring about these benefits.

Yoga and meditation can be excellent tools in fighting panic. They can help panic sufferers to find balance and calmness, and help to bring the body and mind together in a healing way. If you think you may be interested in studying these disciplines, check your yellow pages for schools in your area (look under "Yoga," "Meditation," or "Spirituality").

Positive Thinking

Approaching your life and your problems in a positive way is essential in fighting anxiety and panic. In a way, a panic attack is like a collection of negative thoughts that runs out of control. If you can gain control over your thoughts, you can fight panic more effectively. You have to be able to tell yourself that you can do it.

Pay close attention to your thoughts throughout your day. How often do you tell yourself, "I'm hopeless," "I can't handle this," or "My life is going nowhere"? You

Meditation can help you stay calm and focus your energy in a positive direction.

need to block these negative, self-critical thoughts. Criticizing yourself will get you nowhere. It only makes you feel worse, and bringing about positive change becomes more and more difficult.

Any time you notice that you are beating yourself up or feeling hopeless, tell yourself to stop. Stop right where you are and fight these negative thoughts with positive ones. Say out loud: "I can do this. I am capable. I am strong enough to deal with this." Be confident. Compliment yourself, and believe it. Positive thinking and self-talk can transform your life and are two of the most valuable keys to combating anxiety and panic attacks.

Setting and Approaching Your Goals

The goal of freedom from panic may seem very difficult to reach. After suffering from uncontrollable anxiety and panic attacks for a long time, a person can become discouraged. Conquering these problems sometimes takes an extremely long time and requires a great deal of suffering and struggle. So how does a panic sufferer work toward an end to the pain without losing hope?

The best way to go is one small step at a time. You need to set both long-term and short-term goals. Long-term goals are the big ones. These are the ultimate things you want to accomplish in fighting your problem. But since these goals are so big, you need to create a series of smaller steps in order to get to them. Think of short-term goals as steps on the ladder to success! Each long-term goal has its own series of short-term goals.

You first should figure out what your long-term goals are. You know that you want to be free from panic. But be specific. Are there certain situations or places you avoid out of fear of panic? Do you let anxiety stop you from enjoying life? Are your friendships or classes at school suffering because of panic? Try to narrow down exactly how anxiety and panic are causing problems in your life.

Now take those problems and turn them into goals. For example, a long-term goal may be going out with friends and enjoying yourself without having a panic attack. Or not allowing anxiety to keep you from going to school. Then decide which of these goals will be the most difficult to accomplish.

Now you will set short-term goals to lead you to your long-term goals. Start with one of the least difficult long-term goals to accomplish. Then try to come up with some small step to take that will bring you closer to that goal. For example, let's say your goal is to eat in your favorite restaurant without having a panic attack. A good small step may be walking near the restaurant. Stand across the street from it and try to control any fear that arises.

After one small step is conquered, more ideas for other short-term goals will probably come to you.

Set short-term goals for yourself, breaking down what you wish to do into smaller, more manageable steps.

Perhaps the next step could be standing closer to the restaurant or looking into the window. These goals seem much easier and more possible to achieve than the long-term ones, yet they do take you closer to what you ultimately want to achieve. This is the most effective way to fight panic.

You can also break down your short-term goals into even smaller steps, or tasks, that take you toward the goal itself. For example, if your short-term goal is to make your way toward the restaurant, there are some smaller tasks you can accomplish first to prepare for it. Your first task may be practicing your breathing skills. Then spend half an hour practicing positive self-talk. Relaxation and meditation may be some other tasks you can do first. All of these steps can help you prepare for any short-term goal that you set for yourself.

Taking on your problems one small step at a time may be a bit frustrating because it can be time consuming. But be patient. There is no quick fix in fighting anxiety and panic, but you will be surprised at how good you feel when you start accomplishing those short-term tasks and goals. Before you know it, you'll be well on your way to feeling happy, healthy, and peaceful. It can be a lifelong goal, but it's one you will never regret spending time on.

Glossary

abdominal breathing Method of deep breathing that expands the abdomen (stomach) and aids in relaxation.

agoraphobia Fear of panic, and the places and situations that are associated with it.

anticipatory anxiety Anxiety that is brought on by anticipating a panic attack, usually because of an associated place or situation.

anxiety Fear, worry, or dread.

aspartame Artificial low-calorie sweetener that is said by some to cause side effects, including anxiety and panic attacks.

calm breathing A kind of deep breathing that can help to prevent a panic attack.

debilitated Prevented from functioning in society or from working toward a desired goal.

fight or flight response Instinct brought about by a threatening situation that tells us we have to run away or fight in order to protect ourselves.

generalized anxiety disorder (GAD) Disorder characterized by constant feelings of worry.

instincts Automatic reactions that help to ensure our protection and survival.

irrational fear Fear that occurs even when a situation does not call for it; inappropriate, unprovoked anxiety.

locus coeruleus Part of the brain that regulates breathing and heartbeat.

long-term goals Your ultimate goals in conquering anxiety and panic.

lower lungs Area of the lungs with the most room for air; best to use for deep breathing.

meditation Means of focusing and disciplining the mind through deep relaxation and concentration.

panic attack Collection of negative, frightening thoughts and feelings that becomes out of control; intense fear with no particular object.

panic disorder Disorder characterized by frequent panic attacks.

safe zone Area where an agoraphobic feels safe and protected from anxiety and panic.

short-term goals Smaller steps that move you toward your long-term goals in conquering anxiety and panic.

stigmatized Made to feel excluded, disliked, and/or laughed at.

triggers People, places, and situations that can bring on a panic attack.

yoga Means of focusing and disciplining the mind through deep relaxation, concentration, and holding the body in specially designed poses.

Where to Go for Help

In the United States

American Institute of Stress
124 Park Avenue
Yonkers, NY 10703
(914) 963-1200
e-mail: stress124@earthlink.net
Web site: http://www.stress.org

American Red Cross/Disaster Mental Health Program
Mid America Chapter
43 East Ohio Street
Chicago, IL 60611
(312) 440-2140

Anxiety Disorders Association of America
Rockville, MD 20852
(301) 231-9350
e-mail: anxdis@adaa.com
Web site: http://www.adaa.org

Center for Anxiety and Stress Treatment
4225 Executive Square, Suite 1110
LaJolla, CA 92037
(619) 542-0536
e-mail: health@stressrelease.com
Web site: http://www.stressrelease.com

International Society for Traumatic Stress Studies
60 Revere Drive, Suite 500
Northbrook, IL 60062
(847) 480-9028
e-mail: www@istss.org
Web site: http://www.istss.org

National Anxiety Foundation
3135 Custer Drive
Lexington, KY 40517-4001
(606) 272-7166
Web site: http://www.lexington-online.com/
     naf.html

Panic Disorders Institute
97 West Bellevue Drive
Pasadena, CA 91105
(626) 577-8290
e-mail: shipko@ix.netcom.com
Web site: http://www.algy.com/pdi

In Canada

Anxiety Disorders Association of Ontario
797 Somerset Street West, Suite 14
Ottawa, ON K1R 6R3
(877) 308-3843
e-mail: contactus@anxietyontario.com
Web site: http://www.anxietyontario.com

Canadian Mental Health Association
145 Ontario Street
Stratford, ON N5A 3H1
(519) 273-1391
e-mail: cmha@cyg.net
Web site: http://www.cyg.net/~cmha

Canadian Traumatic Stress Network
3727 Trans-Canada Highway, RR#1
Tappen, BC VOE 2XO

(250) 835-4473
e-mail: ctsn@jetstream.net

Kinark Child and Family Services
240 Duncan Mill Road, Suite 402
Don Mills, ON M3B 3B2
(416) 391-3884
e-mail: info@kinark.on.ca
Web site: http://kinark.on.ca

For Further Reading

Ayer, Eleanor H. *Everything You Need to Know About Stress.* New York: Rosen Publishing Group, 1998.

Ellis, Albert. *How to Control Your Anxiety Before It Controls You.* Secaucus, NJ: Carol Publishing Group, 1998.

Hallowell, Edward M. *Worry: Controlling It and Using It Wisely.* New York: Pantheon Books, 1997.

Kent, Howard. *Breathe Better, Feel Better: Learn to Increase Your Energy, Control Anxiety and Anger, Relieve Health Problems, and Just Relax with Simple Breathing Techniques.* Allentown, PA: People's Medical Society, 1997.

Packard, Gwen. *Coping with Stress.* New York: Rosen Publishing Group, 1999.

Wilson, R. Reid. *Don't Panic: Taking Control of Anxiety Attacks.* New York: Harper Perennial, 1996.

Index

About the Author

John Giacobello is a freelance writer living in New York. He eats lots of guacamole.

Photo Credits

Cover photo by Shalhevet Moshe. All interior shots by Shalhevet Moshe except p. 2 by Les Mills; pp. 8, 23 by Ira Fox; p. 11 by Kristen Artz; p. 20 © Superstock; and p. 31 by Brian Silak.

Layout

Geri Giordano